This book belongs to

_____

I'm on the way!

WHEN MOMMA LEARNED THAT I WAS ON THE WAY _____

_____

_____

_____

WHAT MOMMA SAID TO DADDY _____

_____

_____

_____

HOW DADDY REACTED _____

_____

_____

_____

I AM EXPECTED TO ARRIVE ON THIS DATE _____

_____

The beginning of my story...

From the ultrasound scan it was learned that _____

_____

_____

While waiting for me, Momma and Daddy pictured me as _____

_____

_____

What Momma and Daddy called me when I was in her tummy _____

_____

_____

The hopes and dreams of my parents _____

_____

_____

_____

6

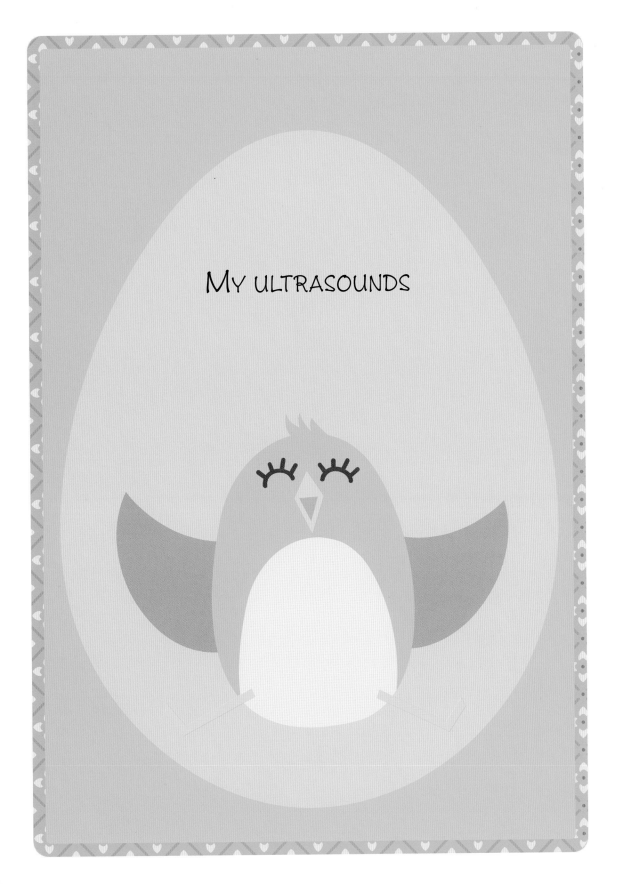

MY ULTRASOUNDS

My parents

MY MOMMA'S
PICTURE

MY DADDY'S
PICTURE

HOW THEY MET ACCORDING TO MOMMA _____

_____

_____

HOW THEY MET ACCORDING TO DADDY _____

_____

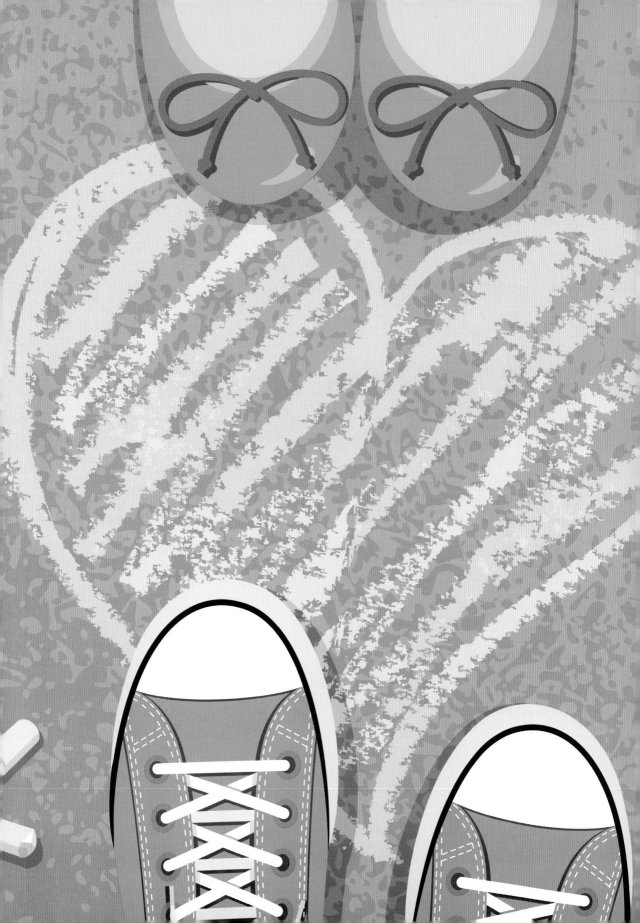

I've arrived!

I WAS BORN ON THIS DATE _____

AT THIS TIME _____

My weight _____

My height _____

I was born at _____

_____

The doctor and the obstetrician present _____

_____

The most vivid memory of the day was _____

_____

_____

My first photograph

Precious memories

A LOCK OF HAIR

THE HOSPITAL
BRACELET

What they said about me...

MOMMA'S FIRST WORDS _____

_____

_____

_____

DADDY'S FIRST WORDS _____

_____

_____

THE HOPES AND GOOD WISHES OF SIBLINGS, GRANDPARENTS, AUNTS AND

UNCLES, AND FRIENDS _____

_____

_____

_____

_____

15

WELL WISHERS' CARDS

  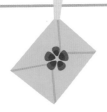 

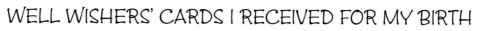

WELL WISHERS' CARDS I RECEIVED FOR MY BIRTH

MY NAME

_____

My name was chosen by _____

_____

_____

What it means _____

_____

_____

My nickname is _____

_____

My identikit

	AT BIRTH
COLOUR OF EYES	
COLOUR OF HAIR	
COMPLEXION	
DISTINGUISHING FEATURES	

AT 6 MONTHS   AT 1 YEAR

MY PHOTOGRAPHS

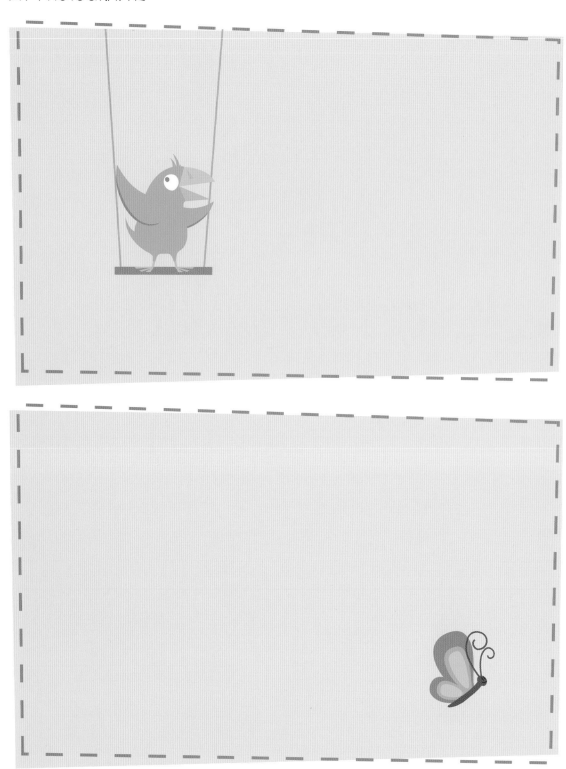

My zodiac sign

ARIES

20 MARCH
20 APRIL

TAURUS

21 APRIL
21 MAY

GEMINI

22 MAY
21 JUNE

CANCER

22 JUNE
22 JULY

LEO

23 JULY
22 AUGUST

VIRGO

23 AUGUST
22 SEPTEMBER

MY ZODIAC SIGN IS

LIBRA

23 SEPTEMBER
22 OCTOBER

SCORPIO

23 OCTOBER
22 NOVEMBER

SAGITTARIUS

23 NOVEMBER
21 DECEMBER

CAPRICORN

22 DECEMBER
20 JANUARY

AQUARIUS

21 JANUARY
19 FEBRUARY

PISCES

20 FEBRUARY
19 MARCH

THE CHARACTERISTICS OF THIS SIGN ARE _____

THE MAIN EVENTS OF THE PERIOD _____

_____

_____

THE HIT SONGS _____

_____

THE MOST POPULAR MOVIES _____

_____

_____

THE BEST-SELLING BOOKS _____

_____

_____

THE WORLD LEADERS ARE _____

_____

SOME CURRENT PRICES _____

_____

World news

My family

MEMBERS OF MY FAMILY _____

_____

_____

28

My momma _____

Her birthday is _____

When she was little she loved _____

_____

_____

My daddy _____

His birthday is _____

When he was little he loved _____

_____

_____

They say I look like...

EYES _____

_____

MOUTH _____

_____

NOSE _____

_____

HAIR _____

_____

EARS _____

_____

DISTINGUISHING FEATURES _____

_____

My family tree

MOMMY

Welcome home !

MY FIRTS ADDRESS

_____

_____

_____

_____

ON THE RIDE HOME

_____

_____

_____

_____

WHO WAS WAITING FOR ME

_____

_____

_____

_____

MY BEDROOM

_____

_____

_____

About the doctor

My pediatrician _____

_____

The first time I went to the doctor _____

_____

My blood type _____

Vaccinations _____

_____

_____

My first illnesses _____

_____

_____

My teeth come through

My first tooth came through _____

How I reacted to my new tooth _____

_____

_____

TOP ROW

LEFT SIDE

RIGHT SIDE

BOTTOM ROW

WRITE IN THE DATE EACH TOOTH COMES THROUGH

See how I'm growing!

	WEIGHT	HEIGHT
AT BIRTH		
ONE MONTH		
TWO MONTHS		
THREE MONTHS		
FOUR MONTHS		
FIVE MONTHS		
SIX MONTHS		
SEVEN MONTHS		
EIGHT MONTHS		
NINE MONTHS		
TEN MONTHS		
ELEVEN MONTHS		
TWELVE MONTHS		
TWO YEARS		
THREE YEARS		

My hand print

My foot print

Wake up, sleepyhead!

HOW I ANNOUNCE THAT I'M AWAKE

MY WAKING UP HABITS

The bath is ready

My first time in the bath _____

_____

_____

_____

How I reacted _____

_____

_____

_____

In the bath I play with _____

_____

_____

_____

My food is ready

My first solid food _____

_____

_____

_____

Momma's recipes _____

_____

_____

_____

_____

_____

_____

_____

My favorite food ....

_____

_____

_____

_____

I don't like ....

_____

_____

_____

_____

Golden dreams

My first night _____

_____

_____

_____

_____

My first whole night's sleep _____

_____

_____

_____

_____

_____

_____

_____

_____

_____

To go to sleep I need...

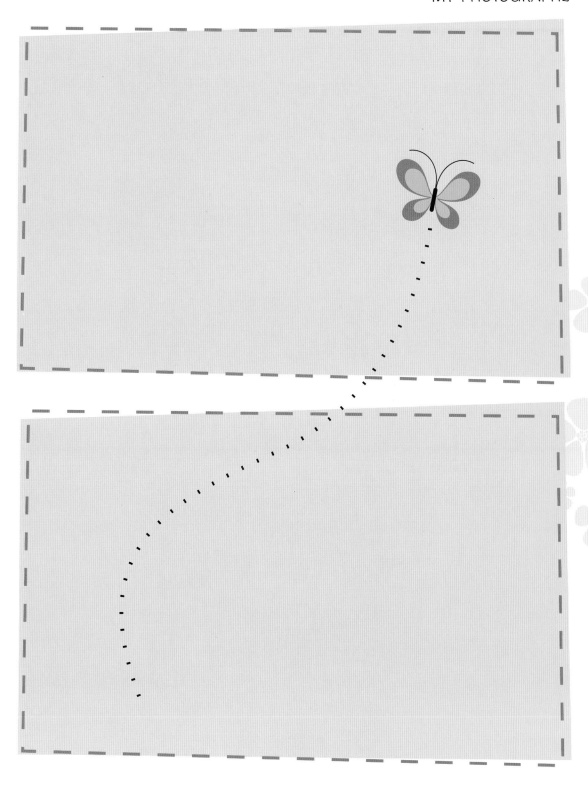

My day

SLEEPING TIMES _____

_____

FEEDING TIMES _____

_____

PLAY TIMES _____

_____

AT THREE MONTHS

SLEEPING TIMES _____

_____

FEEDING TIMES _____

_____

PLAY TIMES _____

_____

AT SIX MONTHS

SLEEPING TIMES _____

_____

FEEDING TIMES _____

_____

PLAY TIMES _____

_____

AT NINE MONTHS

SLEEPING TIMES _____

_____

FEEDING TIMES _____

_____

PLAY TIMES _____

_____

AT TWELVE MONTHS

SLEEPING TIMES _____

_____

FEEDING TIMES _____

_____

PLAY TIMES _____

_____

_____

MUMMY'S MEMORIES _____

_____

_____

_____

_____

My first appearance in public

OUR FAMILY'S FIRST WALK TOOK PLACE _____

_____

_____

_____

_____

_____

HOW I REACTED _____

_____

_____

_____

_____

_____

_____

THE PEOPLE I MET SAID TO ME _____

_____

_____

_____

_____

MY FAVORITE PLACES ARE _____

_____

_____

_____

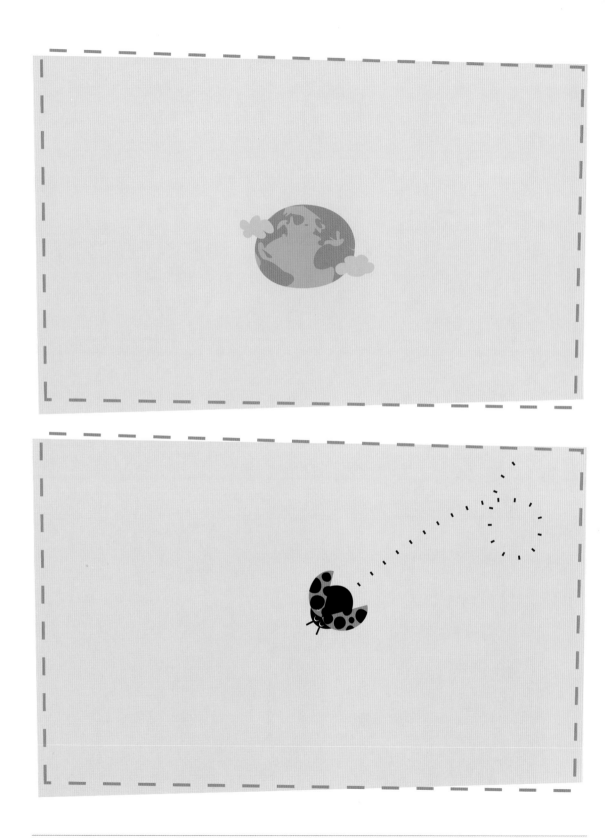

A world to explore

THE FIRST TIME THAT:

I WENT IN AN AUTOMOBILE _____

_____

_____

I WENT ON A TRAIN, AN AIRPLANE OR A SHIP _____

_____

_____

_____

_____

_____

I WENT ON HOLIDAY WITH MY FAMILY _____

_____

_____

I SAW THE SEA _____

_____

_____

I FELT THE SNOW _____

_____

_____

_____

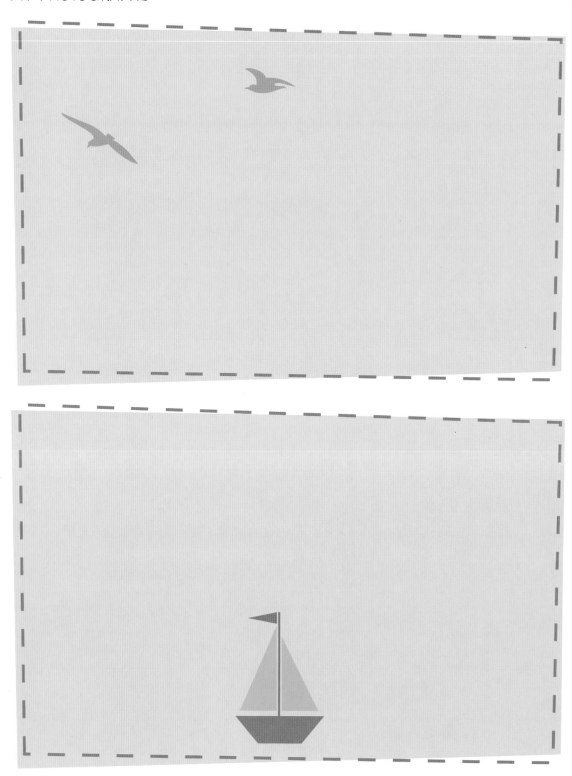

There is always a first time

I SMILED _____

_____

_____

I RECOGNIZED MOMMA AND DADDY _____

_____

_____

I RAISED MY HEAD _____

_____

_____

I SAT UP _____

_____

_____

I GRABBED A TOY _____

_____

_____

I DISCOVERED MY FEET _____

_____

_____

I CLAPPED _____

_____

On the move!

I STARTED CRAWLING _____

_____

I STOOD UP ON MY OWN _____

_____

I WORE MY FIRST "GROWN-UP" SHOES _____

_____

_____

I MADE MY FIRST STEPS WITH A LITTLE HELP

_____

_____

_____

I WALKED ON MY OWN FOR THE FIRST TIME _____

_____

_____

I STARTED DANCING _____

_____

_____

I RAN ON AHEAD ON MY OWN! _____

_____

_____

MY PHOTOGRAPHS

What's my mood

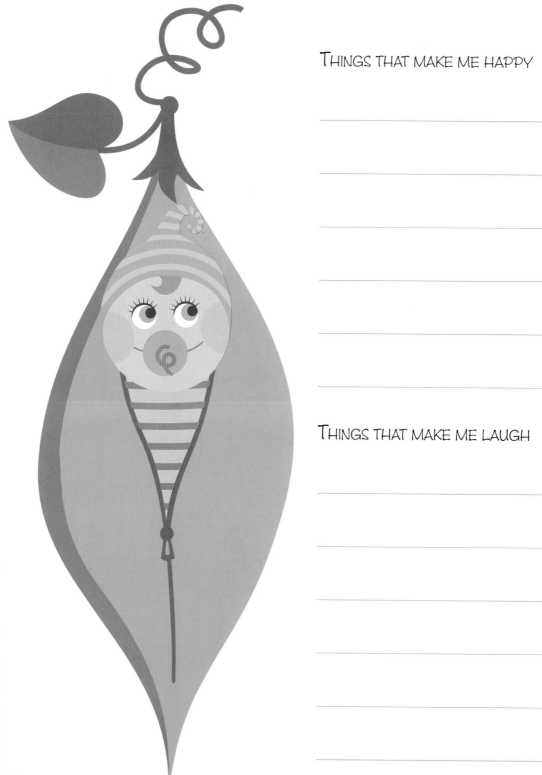

THINGS THAT MAKE ME HAPPY

_____

_____

_____

_____

_____

_____

THINGS THAT MAKE ME LAUGH

_____

_____

_____

_____

_____

THINGS THAT MAKE ME ANGRY

_____

_____

_____

_____

_____

WHAT COMFORTS ME

_____

_____

_____

_____

_____

_____

_____

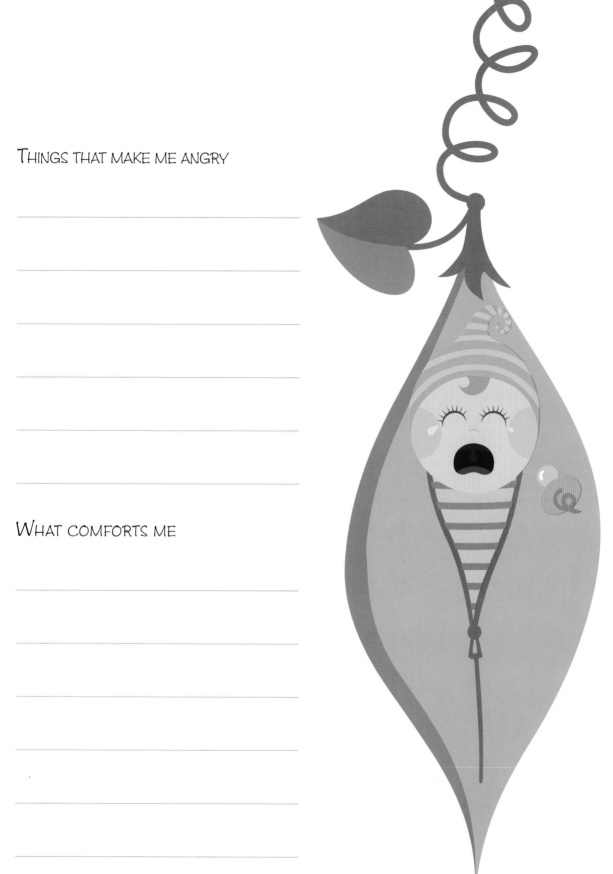

My favorites

Colors _____

_____

Fairy tale characters _____

_____

Clothes _____

_____

Rooms _____

_____

Cartoons _____

_____

Toys _____

_____

Games _____

_____

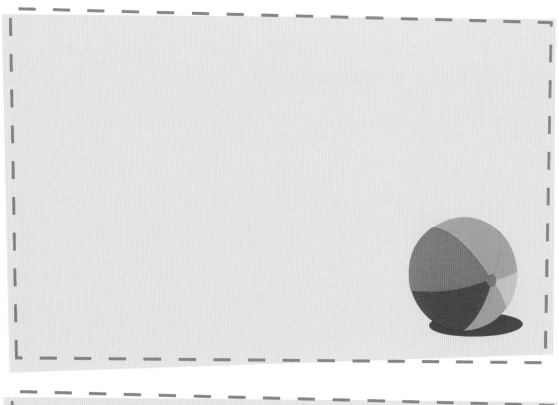

A special day

EVENT _____

_____

_____

WHO WAS THERE _____

_____

_____

_____

AN UNFORGETTABLE MEMORY _____

_____

_____

_____

_____

My first birthday

WHEN AND WHERE THE PARTY TOOK PLACE _____

_____

_____

THE GUESTS _____

_____

_____

MY "LOOK" FOR THE OCCASION _____

_____

GIFTS RECEIVED _____

_____

I REMEMBER THAT _____

_____

_____

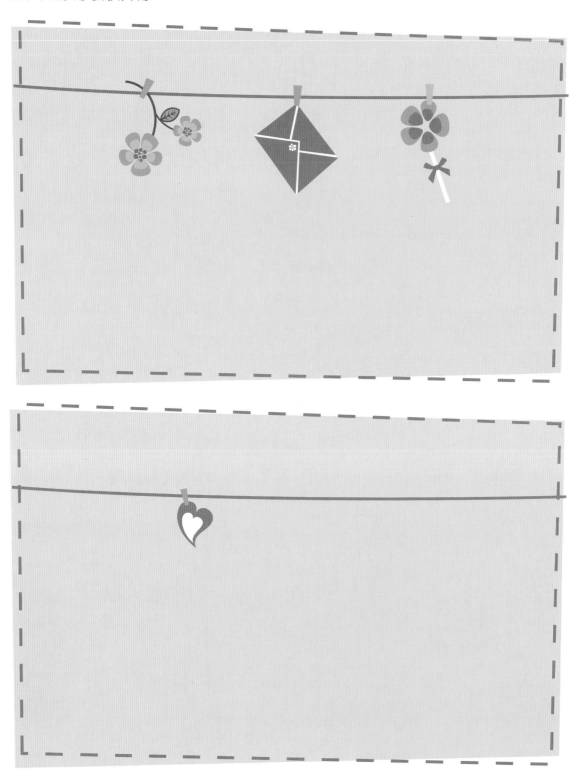

ONE
YEAR
OLD!

IN THE LAST 12 MONTHS MOMMA AND DADDY HAVE NEVER FORGOTTEN

THE TIME WHEN I... _____

_____

_____

_____

WHAT I LEARNED TO DO THIS YEAR _____

_____

_____

_____

MY PERSONALITY _____

_____

_____

_____

HOW MUCH I HAVE GROWN IN ONE YEAR

WEIGHT _____ HEIGHT _____

My favorites!

FAIRY TALE _____

SONG _____

TOY _____

CARTOON _____

STUFFED ANIMAL _____

GAME _____

GARMENT _____

THE THING THAT MAKES ME HAPPIEST _____

_____

THE THING THAT MAKES ME UPSET _____

_____

THE THING THAT COMFORTS ME _____

_____

_____

There is always a first time

I BUILT A TOWER _____

_____

I TRIED TO GET DRESSED ON MY OWN _____

_____

I ATE ON MY OWN _____

_____

I THREW A BALL IN THE AIR _____

_____

I JUMPED _____

_____

MY NEW EXPERIENCES _____

A
B
C

_____

_____

_____

Famous
first words

THE FIRST WORD I SPOKE WAS _____

_____

HOW I PRONOUNCED IT _____

_____

_____

_____

_____

I SAID "MOMMA" FOR THE FIRST TIME _____

_____

_____

_____

I SAID "DADDY" FOR THE FIRST TIME _____

_____

_____

_____

A special day

EVENT _____

_____

WHO WAS THERE _____

_____

_____

_____

_____

AN UNFORGETTABLE MEMORY _____

_____

_____

_____

_____

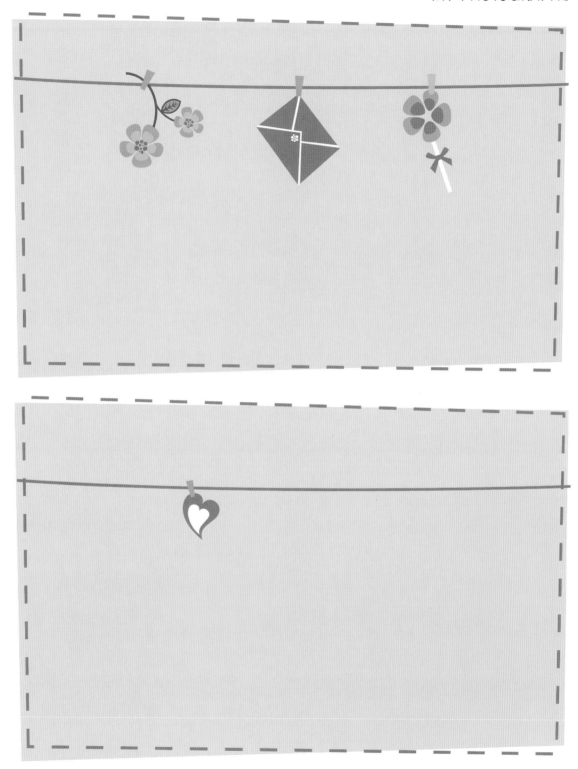

Traveling!

OUR DESTINATION _____

_____

_____

SOMETHING WE SAW _____

_____

_____

HOW I BEHAVED _____

_____

_____

A SPECIAL MEMORY _____

_____

_____

_____

MY PHOTOGRAPHS

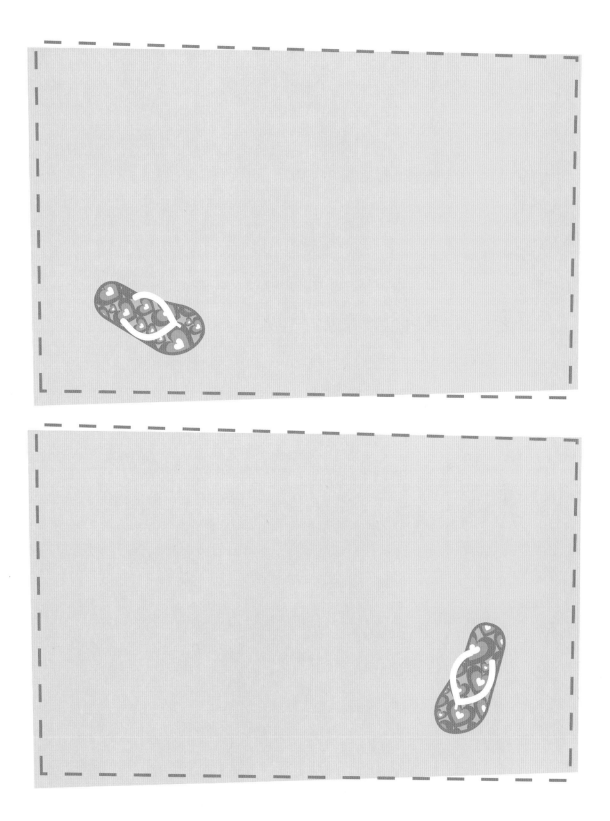

My second birthday

WHEN AND WHERE THE PARTY TOOK PLACE _____

_____

MY "LOOK" FOR THE OCCASION _____

_____

_____

GIFTS RECEIVED _____

_____

_____

_____

I REMEMBER THAT_____

_____

_____

_____

THE GUESTS

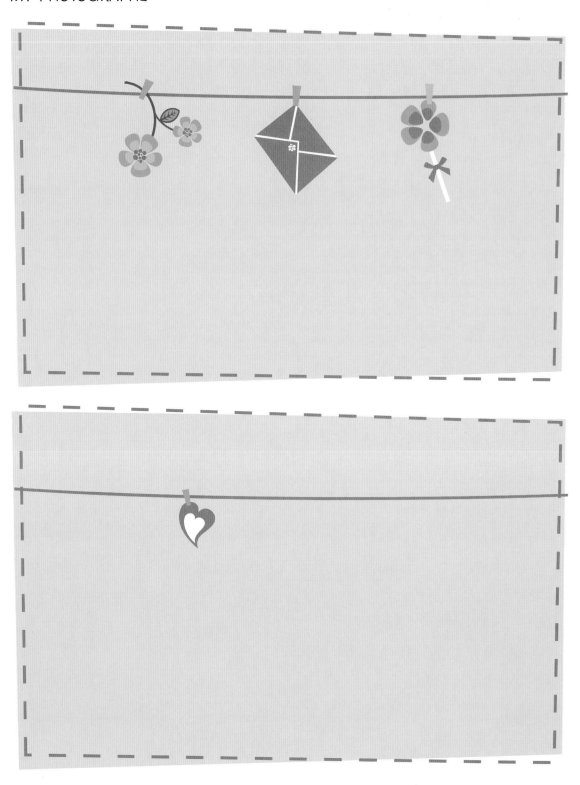

TWO
YEARS
OLD

IN THE LAST 12 MONTHS MOMMA AND DADDY HAVE NEVER FORGOTTEN

THE TIME WHEN I... _____

_____

_____

_____

WHAT I LEARNED TO DO THIS YEAR _____

_____

_____

_____

MY PERSONALITY _____

_____

_____

_____

HOW MUCH I HAVE GROWN IN ONE YEAR

WEIGHT _____ HEIGHT _____

My favorites!

FAIRY TALE _____

SONG _____

TOY _____

CARTOON _____

STUFFED ANIMAL _____

GAME _____

_____

GARMENT _____

THE THING THAT MAKES ME HAPPIEST _____

_____

THE THING THAT MAKES ME UPSET _____

_____

THE THING THAT COMFORTS ME _____

_____

_____

There is always a first time

I STOPPED WEARING DIAPERS _____

I DREW A CIRCLE _____

I RECOGNIZED COLORS _____

I COUNTED UP TO FIVE _____

I BRUSHED MY TEETH MYSELF _____

I RODE A TRYCICLE _____

I DRESSED ON MY OWN _____

I USED MY OWN NAME _____

A NEW EXPERIENCE _____

_____

_____

_____

_____

A special day

Event _____

_____

Who was there _____

_____

_____

_____

_____

An unforgettable memory _____

_____

_____

_____

_____

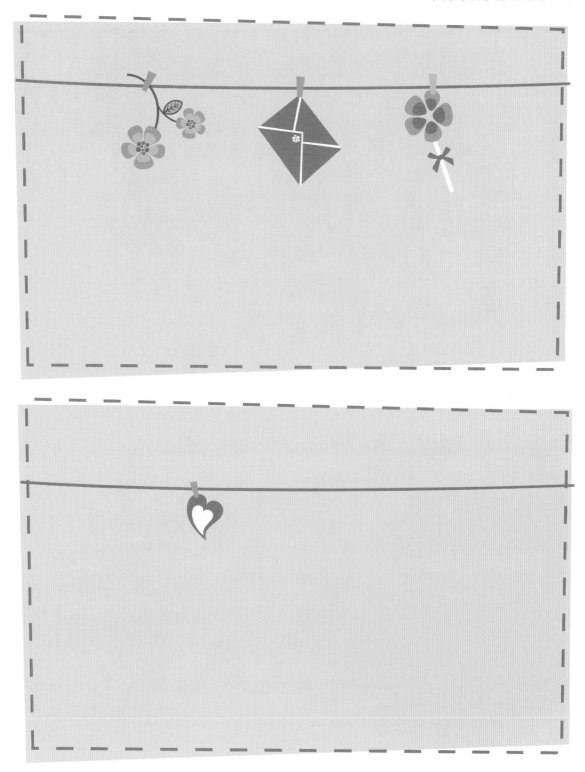

Traveling!

OUR DESTINATION _____

_____

_____

SOMETHING WE SAW _____

_____

_____

_____

_____

_____

_____

_____

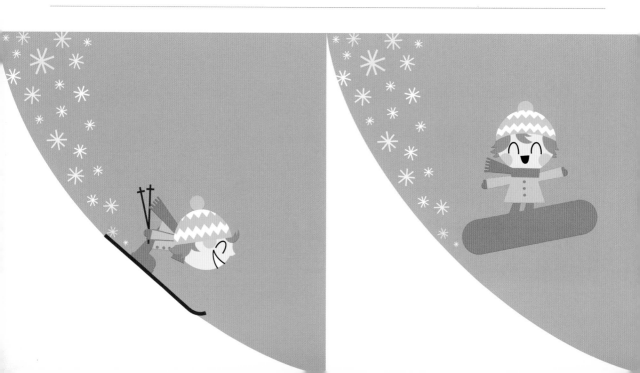

How I behaved _____

_____

_____

_____

_____

A special memory _____

_____

_____

_____

_____

MY PHOTOGRAPHS

My third birthday!

When and where the party took place _____

_____

The guests _____

_____

_____

My "look" for the occasion _____

_____

Gifts received _____

_____

_____

I remember that _____

_____

_____

MY PHOTOGRAPHS

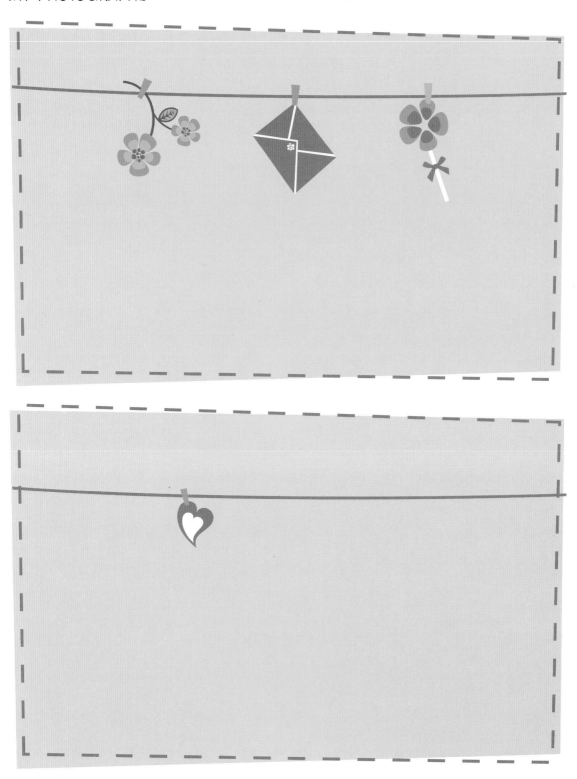

THREE
YEARS
OLD

IN THE LAST 12 MONTHS MOMMA AND DADDY HAVE NEVER FORGOTTEN

THE TIME WHEN I... _____

_____

_____

_____

WHAT I LEARNED TO DO THIS YEAR _____

_____

_____

_____

MY PERSONALITY _____

_____

_____

_____

HOW MUCH I HAVE GROWN IN ONE YEAR

WEIGHT _____ HEIGHT _____

My favorites!

Fairy tale _____

Song _____

Toy _____

Cartoon _____

Stuffed animal _____

Game _____

Garment _____

The thing that makes me happiest _____

_____

The thing that makes me upset _____

_____

The thing that comforts me _____

_____

There is always a first time

I DREW A PICTURE OF AN ANIMAL

I WENT TO A FRIEND'S PARTY

I CHOSE MY CLOTHES IN THE MORNING

I WROTE MY OWN NAME

I STOPPED USING A PACIFIER

My first time at preschool

THE TEACHER _____

_____

_____

_____

MY FAVORITE GAMES _____

_____

_____

_____

MY REACTIONS _____

_____

_____

_____

Friends...

My new friends are called _____

_____

_____

_____

With them I play these games _____

_____

_____

_____

MY BEST FRIEND IS

....

MY BEST FRIEND'S BIRTHDAY IS

....

WITH MY BEST FRIEND I PLAY ....

....

....

Traveling!

OUR DESTINATION ....

....

....

SOMETHING WE SAW ....

....

....

HOW I BEHAVED ....

....

....

A SPECIAL MEMORY ....

....

....

....

MY PHOTOGRAPHS